The P⬥wer
of
Ownership

The continuing tale about the importance
of taking control in business and in life.

The P**●**wer *of* Ownership

Making a choice.

MICHAEL D. KHOURI

A D PROFESSIONAL DEVELOPMENT PUBLISHING
Lake Ann, Michigan

AD PROFESSIONAL DEVELOPMENT PUBLISHING
Lake Ann, Michigan

ISBN: 978-09796809-1-5 | LCCN: 2016951381

Michael Khouri is available for training and speaking engagements, and consultations to individuals and groups. To inquire about his availability, contact him at: **michaelkhouri.com**.

Manufactured in the United States of America
First Edition

Cover and text design by Mary Jo Zazueta
tothepointsolutions.com

CONTENTS

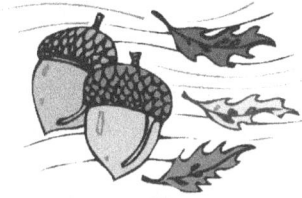

PREFACE

The Power of Ownership—In a Nutshell Series was given birth by a seminar I wrote in 2005 that evolved into the book *15 Ways to Own Your Future,* which was released in the fall of 2016. *Book 2, Making a Choice*, continues the saga of Uni, Unkno, and Untra, three squirrels from Upheaval.

In book 1, Uni, Unkno, and Untra experienced adversity and chaos because they have chosen to not make choices or decisions. The message was that we do own what we do or decide not to do, and that non-decisions are really decisions.

In book 2, we find these three squirrels trying to recover from a horrifying storm that has thrown them to parts unknown. They begin to realize the adverse consequences that continually result from not taking ownership. They have seen the impact that no effort, no defined purpose, and lack of planning does to even the simplest existence.

In *Making a Choice*, Uni, Unkno, and Untra reach a crossroad. They finally realize that a change in perspective might open up new opportunities that before were not possible. And that they must either make decisions that shape their lives or perpetuate the upheaval that has defined their existence.

Like Uni, Unkno, and Untra, we too are confronted daily by minor and significant adversity and challenges, in business and in life. We are faced with the choice of either making a decision or simply ignoring what is happening and do nothing. At some point, we either attempt to take control and look forward, or we resign ourselves to perpetually being swept away by the next storm. In resignation, we accept (choose) that we will simply take what comes.

The P🌰wer

of
Ownership

Chapter One

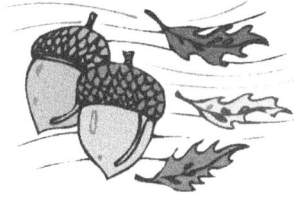

Upheaval Revisited

Going through the motions is
like operating in the dark.

Three days ago, a great storm tossed Uni,
Unkno, and Untra from Upheaval. Since then, they
have been wandering with no destination in mind;
and as such, no destination has been reached. They
do not know where they are or where they are
headed. Their noncommittal approach and lackadai-
sical traveling has made the days seem like months.

Even though their landing had a feeling of
upheaval to it—normalcy for them—oddly, they
were not comforted. It was one thing to live in

familiar upheaval; yet quite another to experience new upheaval and not understand it. These unattached, uninterested little squirrels are confused and traumatized.

Life was not good. After three days of not knowing where they were going or why, or if it mattered, Uni, Unkno, and Untra began to realize there just may be another way to approach life.

Uni, whose full name was Unintentional because of his total lack of intent, began to intentionally wonder what taking an interest in life might accomplish, as opposed to just accepting what came their way. It was one thing to be accustomed to being a victim of events; it was altogether another to perpetually enjoy the results.

Unkno, whose full name was Unknowingly because of his continual lack of acknowledgement, began to consider the possible rewards of being aware. What would have happened if they had given adverse events the recognition each deserved? Could they have limited the chaos in their lives that resulted from their apathy?

Untra, whose full name was Untrained because of his lack of training and desire for training, began to wonder what their lives might be like if they had opened themselves up to learning.

We become wiser by adversity;
prosperity destroys our
appreciation of the right.

SENECA

Chaos is merely order waiting to be deciphered.

JOSE SARAMAGO

Upon reaching a large bush they had already passed many times, they abruptly came to a stop and looked at each other. Even though they were exhausted, they realized this was actually their first attempt at communicating. They had never done this before. They had lived most of their lives blindly bound by a common lack of interest.

Had they finally had enough chaos in their lives? Not necessarily. But what had suddenly become clear to each of them was that this approach of not taking control by making choices was becoming tiring, irritating, and completely draining.

Having doubts about how they had chosen to live their lives was significant. To have any thought on any issue was a monumental milestone for these lazy, uninterested squirrels.

Could making an effort be less exhausting than their total disregard for making choices? At the very least, considering their choices and making a decision might reduce some of the exhausting results. How much more tired could they be by showing some interest and trying to make an impact on their lives? It certainly could not be any worse. They had seen a lifetime of worse.

Passing by the bush, for what felt like the hundredth time, made a major impression on these beat and battered squirrels. Even they could not miss the symbolism. This walking in circles and lack of progress had taken them to a lower level than they had ever been before. Not only had it taken a toll on them physically, it had taken a major toll on them mentally, and that was saying a lot!

Coming to a sudden stop at the same time was quite a sight. It was the closest to communicating these friends had ever experienced. They were actually synchronized! Granted, it was synchronization at its weakest, but it was synchronization just the same.

You could say they had been doing this for years. After all they had always lived in the same area doing nothing together. But doing nothing for no reason is totally different than doing nothing intentionally. Being together because of inaction and a shared lack of effort, which resulted in them living in the same location, was different than purposefully living together.

At this moment, these three squirrels were finally making an effort to take inventory of their situation. It could be argued that they had experienced the revelation that it was time to reflect and learn. As daunting as this was to their lazy brains, they stopped in unison and glared at each other.

No one and nothing outside of you can give you salvation, or free you from the misery. You have to light your own lamp. You have to know the miniature universe that you yourself are.

BANANI RAY, *AWAKENING INNER GURU*

This glaring continued for several hours. This major step toward communication was monumental and had to be taken slowly. Someone would have to commit to speaking. Who that would be, was not going to be quickly determined.

How could Uni speak first, when he had never done anything intentionally in his life? How could Unkno speak first, since knowingly doing anything was not something he had ever done? And who would expect Untra to speak first, since he was not trained to say something that might define any situation?

Uni broke the silence. "I believe we have unintentionally been going around in circles for days," he stated.

"Do you know that to be fact?" Unkno spat out with a gulp.

"How did you learn that?" asked Untra.

Uni could not answer these questions—nor did Unkno or Untra—because they were not used to analysis and they certainly were not accustomed to responding to questions.

After a long pause, they started to gesture and grunt as they circled the bush. This limited exchange was a small step toward what might eventually result in verbal communication. They had made

Remember, a real decision is measured by the fact that you've taken new action. If there's no action, you haven't truly decided.

ANTHONY ROBBINS

Not everything that is faced can be changed, but nothing can be changed until it is faced.

JAMES BALDWIN

great progress. First there was the synchronized stop and glare, and they each had made an intentional acknowledgement and evaluation that could lead to learning. They were beginning to feel enlightened.

Suddenly a huge smile appeared on their faces; and then, all at once, statements and questions began to fire out of their mouths in exhilarating screams like bullets from a machine gun.

After three days of walking in a daze, suddenly, it was like a magic wand had been waved over them. It was as though they had woken up from a long, deep sleep. For the first time ever, they shared their thoughts. They had finally realized things had to change. They did not know how they were going to do that as yet. They did not know what they were going to change. What they did know was that it was time for change.

"Do you think we should try to stop going in circles and set a course?" asked Unkno, jumping as though he had seen a ghost.

"I think we should intentionally do that," said Uni, gulping as though he had swallowed a frog.

"I think we may be able to learn something that could end this going around in circles," said Untra, shaking his head in amazement at what had just come out of his mouth.

Chapter Two

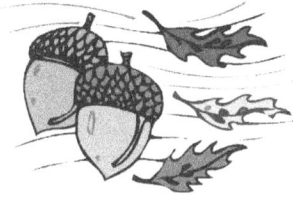

A Little Rat ... ionality

*We can learn a lot by just being open
to listening and observing others.*

After about an hour of getting familiar with interacting and exchanging ideas, Uni, Unkno, and Untra came to a life-altering conclusion: they would indeed change their ways. They were so excited by this release of communication that had been stored up for years. They were even more excited about their ability to reason—which they had never realized they had. They held hands and jumped up and down while letting out screeches that could be heard in regions far away.

After thirty minutes of synchronized screeching, it occurred to the squirrels that this unified celebration may have felt good, but it was clearly not advancing their agenda. Uni realized that standing together in exhilaration may have been intentional, but their real intention was to move forward. Unkno realized that this acknowledgment may have been a great revelation, but that awareness would not be beneficial without some form of action. And Untra recognized that even though their knowledge may have been advanced through this understanding, knowledge is undervalued if it is not utilized.

So much analysis was giving these little squirrels a headache—and they now had to figure out how to advance this euphoria to the next step. It was time to move forward, but where? What would their next revelation be?

Uni thought hard, hoping to intentionally come up with a direction they should take. It occurred to Unkno that it was indeed time to decide on a direction. And Untra, knew it was time to put this new, yet limited, knowledge to a test.

It was one thing to think about doing something; it was altogether another to determine a direction. It was clearly something else to actually take steps forward; so, they just walked hand in hand, hoping that something would trigger a thought that might help them decide on a direction.

Making a choice was a new phenomenon for them. They not only lacked experience, but they had not an ounce of understanding. They were not prepared for any kind of change to their behavior. They had never made it a practice to intentionally do anything. They had never knowingly created a plan for any kind of action. The thought of intellectual development and character growth was preposterous.

How would they begin to learn, when learning was something they were unaccustomed to and had never considered?

They decided they would just continue walking in one direction along a narrow, leafy path and see where it took them. This path was bordered by scratchy bushes that the seasonal weather had been abusing for weeks. One could easily see these bushes were losing their vibrant green color and blossoms.

After what seemed like days of walking and resting whenever they became tired, they came to a riverbank. Upon getting closer, they sniffed in unison at an aroma that caused them to pause and stop in a synchronized formation. They gazed in amazement at the activity they witnessed near a tranquil, flowing stream.

Any fool can know. The point is to understand.

ALBERT EINSTEIN

It was a family of rats that not only appeared to be dancing in euphoric ecstasy, but also showing an affectionate appreciation of one another in the process. These rats clearly felt an attachment to each other, and they were not shy about showing it.

Some small rats were chasing each other and wrestling, while a large rat watched and cheered in approval. As this play was going on, there was another rat that appeared to be hunting in the stream for small fish. Without warning, another group of rats appeared from the other side of the stream and joined in the festivities. The one exception was a pudgy rat that joined the rat who was trying to catch fish.

This certainly was more activity than Uni, Unkno, and Untra were accustomed to focusing on. It almost made them too dizzy to watch. In a mesmerized state, they perked up their ears and listened.

The largest rat's name was Greta, and Greta referred to the pudgy rat as Studi.

"It sure is neat to see the family together and the kids having fun and enjoying each other's company," Greta exclaimed in a satisfying tone.

"It doesn't get any better than this," Studi agreed. "However," Studi added, "we can't just sit here and watch. We should catch some fish and gather enough seeds for dinner and add to our supplies for the upcoming winter. Heard there might be some pretty rough weather ahead of us.

"If you study the weather patterns we have been experiencing and you accelerate those patterns, they equate to climate challenges ahead; we must prepare accordingly."

"Even though I always have a great appreciation for the present, we should always take time to look toward the future. I don't ever doubt your keen sense and grasp for looking forward," Greta said, in an appreciative and admiring tone. "Are you concerned about the challenges you think might come our way?" Greta added.

"It does not matter so much that there will be major challenges. If we are prepared and anticipate like we should, I couldn't give a rat's butt about how difficult the challenges may be," Studi answered with a slight snicker.

As Studi and Greta laughed, Uni, Unkno, and Untra looked at each other inquisitively. Why were the large rats laughing at what Studi had just said? "Rat's butt?" they stated in unison.

As the younger rats continued to play and Greta and Studi continued to swim for fish, Uni, Unkno, and Untra watched in amazement at all that was going on in this community of rats.

You never achieve real success
unless you like what you are doing.
DALE CARNEGIE

Uni was amazed at the intentional enjoyment and play of the rats, and the intentional affection they had for one another. He could not help but be impressed by Greta and Studi, who stayed focused on catching fish and looking for seeds. Greta and Studi were dedicated in their intent. They were on a mission for the family.

Unkno could not believe the knowledge that both Greta and Studi possessed; especially Studi's ability to evaluate the past and the present. The rats knew what they had to do and they knew why they had to do it. Unkno was also impressed with their ability to put that knowledge to work for a cause. And he was astounded at Greta's appreciation for life. He wondered how she had come by it.

Untra felt a little envious of all that Greta and Studi had learned. He wondered if this understanding was something they were just born with. He also wondered how much of it had taken time and experience to acquire. What he found to be even more surprising was the trust each of these rats had in one another. He could not imagine how long it had taken to develop that relationship.

The three squirrels continued to observe the rats and their interaction with one another. It must have been a common occurrence for them because it looked so natural. It was just business and life as usual.

Suddenly Uni, Unkno, and Untra were startled out of their mesmerized state by the rapid movement of the little rats as they scurried into the bushes behind them. With their cheeks puffed full of seeds, the rats quickly marched, one by one, into a nearby burrow. Then they reappeared, with their cheeks slack, and scurried into the bushes again. While repeating this process over and over, the rats gave each other high fives and commended each other on a job well done. It was evident to the squirrels that although the rats were working, they also took time to show appreciation to each other.

While watching the rats gather and store food, the now attentive squirrels also noticed a few snakes near the riverbank. Studi and Greta were also aware of the snakes and kept an eye on them. It was well understood by these rats that snakes were their natural enemy, and that the riverbank was a spawning ground for snakes. But the river area was a haven for small fish and bushes that produced seeds. It was a risk they knew they had to take in order to survive, so that's what they did. The rats understood that anything worthwhile of achieving carried risks.

Uni recognized the presence of the snakes, but

Small things start us in new ways
of thinking.

V.S. NAIPAUL, *A BEND IN THE RIVER*

was unsure if the rats intentionally lived in this area. Unkno was not sure if the rats knew the snakes were present or if they knew and did not care. Untra could not figure out if the rats had ever learned of the potential danger of living near snakes.

What these squirrels were beginning to understand was getting clearer and clearer by the hour. They had been observing the rats for more than half a day. These rats loved life, loved getting things done, loved each other, and were willing to take risks.

It was near sunset and time for the squirrels to move on in search of a safe place to spend the night.

As they turned their backs on the rats, Uni spoke first. "I'm glad we intentionally took the time to observe the rats today; I believe we may have witnessed some great intent."

Unkno added, "I think I know what I saw; they seemed to know what they were doing, that's for sure."

Untra responded with a smirk, "I couldn't give a rats butt what we may have intentionally done or if we know why those rats did what they did—but, I think I actually learned something today by all that observing!"

After a short pause, the three squirrels looked at each other and laughed in unison.

Chapter Three

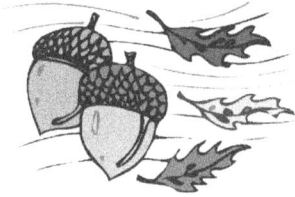

EYE SEE

Taking a chance is not easy;
it's a lot like achievement in that way.

Uni, Unkno, and Untra realized they only had a couple hours before the sun would set and it would be too dark for travel. They had learned this while wandering for days. And, they also knew it was time to decide on a direction.

At that moment, they did something they had never done before: they had a quick discussion about what direction they should take! Uni was clear on one thing. He wanted to make sure the path they took would be intentional. Unkno was convinced they should know which direction to take; and he hoped their decision would be knowledge-based. And Untra believed what they had learned over the last few days would help them determine a direction.

With all that was understood by these bonding squirrels, they decided to take Untra's lead and follow the sun. So, using the setting sun as their short-term guide, they headed westward.

After walking for quite a distance, they stopped in a small village that had many trees and inhabited burrows. The abundance of trees made it difficult for them to decide which tree to homestead for the night.

While sitting at the base of a mid-sized tree that was full of nuts and seeds, Unkno and Untra realized something they had never noticed before. If it had not been so exhilarating, it would have been frightening. (Had what they observed that day awakened their senses?) What a sight it was!

Unkno and Untra were shocked to realize that Uni was a very tall squirrel; at least a head taller than the two of them. They also noticed Uni had a pink nose and slender frame. He was tall and skinny. When he smiled, which they had not noticed before, he showed a little dimple in his chin.

Know yourself to improve yourself.
AUGUSTE COMTE

Uni's teeth sparkled. He must have been smiling in response to Unkno's and Untra's intentional glare. Uni begun to strut like a model on a catwalk, fully realizing it was intentional. He was enjoying the attention.

Uni and Untra turned their attention to Unkno, and noticed that he also appeared to be a tremendous specimen of a squirrel. Unkno had a purple stripe that ran down the full length of his back. His back lit up as he walked. His face was perfectly egg-shaped. His eyes were perfectly rounded. They were eyes that seemed appropriate; a perfect match for his nose that sparkled when he talked.

When standing, Unkno projected a presence of expertise and knowledge. Unkno took a step back, uncomfortable by the hypnotic stare coming from his two friends. Unkno would have given almost anything to know what they saw as they focused on his majestic presence.

Next Uni and Unkno turned their attention to Untra; and they were not disappointed in what they saw. Untra was a solid squirrel from head to toe. Not as tall as Uni, Untra was, however, slightly taller than Unkno. Untra was not as slim as Uni, and not as majestic looking as Unkno, but he was extremely athletic looking. Uni and Unkno knew in a minute that if they were ever in danger, having Untra in their corner would improve their odds of survival.

Uni and Unkno smiled in admiration; Untra appreciated the command his stature deserved. With Untra by their side, they felt secure and safe from any unwanted and unfriendly guests.

Untra not only had a solid torso, he had the muscle to go with that torso. His muscles bulged. When he walked, the ground moved out of respect. For once in his life, at least for as long as he could remember, watching his two friends stare with respect was a learning moment. He learned that he must be something special if others felt in awe of him. It made him feel good.

They made the decision to take a risk and spend the night in the tree. After all, the rats had shown them that risk-taking was paramount to survival, and a stepping stone to achievement in life. They reasoned that meeting challenges could produce some rewards.

Individually, they had gained confidence from the day's activities; and, most importantly, after realizing the qualities each possessed, they felt strong as a team. Uni, with his magnificent height and slender frame, would protect them by being able to see into the distance. Unkno, with his impressive presence,

Life is inherently risky. There
is only one big risk you should
avoid at all costs, and that is the
risk of doing nothing.

DENIS WAITLEY

radiant look of knowledge, and purple glow, would mesmerize anyone who came near. And Untra's athletic frame would make even the most fearless predator cautious before approaching them.

As their newfound appreciation of each other's strengths took hold, they wondered why others who they had come in contact with in Upheaval had not seen what they now saw.

Although these squirrels had come a long way in a few days, they knew there was more to learn. They hoped that at one point they would discover the answer to that question.

For now, it was time to get some sleep. If tomorrow was anything like the day they had just experienced, they would need their rest. They were tired.

As they settled in a burrow near the base of the tree, they did not know where they were. The only thing they knew for certain was they weren't in Upheaval. And maybe that was not such a bad thing.

Chapter Four

ALTER THE DAMN SURROUNDINGS

Don't just take what you are given; always be ready to take it to another level.

Morning came quickly as the three squirrels were awakened by the sound of biting, followed by a shearing squeal, a quick wince, and sudden silence.

Uni was the first to stand up and peer into the distance, his tall frame giving him the ability to look over bushes and leaves. He wondered if the eerie sound was an intentional act to scare them from the burrow at the base of the tree they had inhabited for the night. Intentional or not, the sight of scattered fur rugs along the landscape was discomforting.

Unkno saw Uni intentionally looking out over the horizon and wanted to know what he was missing. It did not take him long to figure out what Uni was staring at. He too saw the fur rugs scattered around the area.

Untra quickly jumped up and sprinted about fifty feet from the tree. He could not help but notice the abundance of fur rugs. Untra knew he was learning something new. He had certainly never seen anything like this before; although, it could be he had simply never observed his surroundings before.

What was clear to all of them was that there had been a great deal of activity during the night. What they also realized, with their fresh eyes after a good night's sleep, was the nearby number of mature trees. This area was a haven of forest habitat unlike any they had ever seen. There were trees as far as they could see. Because they arrived near sunset, Uni, Unkno, and Untra had not realized the magnificent magnitude of the forest.

They could hear the constant rustle of birds flying and the unrelenting sound of chirping. These three squirrels had slept so soundly, they had not heard some of the earlier activity emanating from the forest village of Oodles.

It was time to take a walk around Oodles and survey their surroundings. With their new interest in observation, they began to walk around Oodles. It was a vibrant area that offered an abundance of nuts and seeds. It was enough food to feed an army of squirrels. There would be no fear of going hungry here.

As they stopped to eat, their ears perked up. They heard running water and the sound of teeth gnawing on wood. Then they heard a loud splash as a small tree hit the pond. These sounds were different than what they had heard yesterday while watching the rats.

Uni, Unkno, and Untra positioned themselves to view the activity. What a sight it was. Several beavers were busy transforming the area into a functional homestead. They were changing the landscape to fit their needs.

Uni, Unkno, and Untra were confused about what the beavers were trying to accomplish. Were they creating an environment for protection? Were they creating a food source? Or, were they trying to attract visitors? It appeared they might have been

The people who get on in this world are the people who get up and look for the circumstances they want, and, if they can't find them, make them.

GEORGE BERNARD SHAW

trying to accomplish all of these things because the squirrels noticed a variety of waterfowl and insects nearby.

Although the squirrels had made tremendous progress transitioning from an apathetic existence to a sense of awareness, they were not at the point where they felt comfortable making inquiries. However, they were comfortable asking each other about their observations. "Are these busy, hardworking beavers intentionally reforming this area, or is it an unintentional result?" asked Uni.

"It appears to me that they know what they are doing because a lot of good things are happening," Unkno replied. "And I don't think the results can just be happenstance."

"I wonder if these guys just learned this or if someone had to teach them? Or is this just knowledge they were born with," asked Untra.

These were great questions that portrayed the fact they were paying attention. As they continued their vigilant observation, the squirrels noticed what appeared to be a den underneath a log. The inhabitant looked different; it was not a beaver. The beavers must have been aware he was there because they made no effort to encourage the visitor to leave. This observation made no sense to the vigilant squirrels.

Success is not final, failure is not fatal: it is the courage to continue that counts.

WINSTON CHURCHILL

The hours passed and the temperature began to drop. The squirrels sensed it was time to return to their new home and decide on a course of action for the night. So, they turned around and started to walk back to the tree they had settled in the previous night.

They knew they were getting close when they saw fur rugs lying on the ground. As they spotted their burrow, they noticed a small, white animal standing on its heels peering out at them. He did not look friendly, but they continued toward the burrow just the same.

The animal had a small, narrow head that was not much thicker than its neck. His body was slender and his legs were short. He had a sharply pointed snout; triangular head; small, rounded ears; and beady black eyes. His head was a dark color. The dark color ran from its head, to its back, and continued to his legs and tail. His belly was clearly exposed as he stood on his hind legs. His belly was white.

As they approached, the animal began to snort and hiss. It also made a chirping sound. Suddenly, he started to go into a rhythmic dance. He began to hop back and forth and his tail frizzed up. This was turning into a bad situation.

Chapter Five

Standing Tall

> To conquer a challenge, you must
> first be willing to meet it head-on.

The Uni, Unkno, and Untra of Upheaval

would have immediately run the other way. They
would never have considered confronting the bel-
ligerent character standing between them and their
home. In fact, in Upheaval, the squirrels would not
have put themselves in any situation with this potential for conflict and risk.

The intruder was quite the intimidating weasel—
not a foe any sensible squirrel would ever consider

Our doubts are traitors, and
make us lose the good we oft
might win, by fearing to attempt.

WILLIAM SHAKESPEARE

confronting. As the squirrels slowly neared, the weasel began to chirp louder and louder.

Uni, Unkno, and Untra did not consider what their immediate intentions were. They certainly did not know the danger they were approaching. And they were definitely not trained for the combat that most assuredly was forthcoming.

Without realizing his actions, Uni glared at the weasel, his pink nose shining in defiance. Uni stood much taller than the weasel, and the gleam from his teeth nearly overshadowed his tall stature.

Unkno stood as straight as Uni, and the purple stripe down his back lit up the area and enhanced the magnificence of the perfect specimen he was. He too was taller than the weasel.

Untra stared down the weasel, and his impressive, athletic frame looked ready for battle. Untra looked like a professional wrestler getting ready to take on a lightweight, a clear mismatch for Untra's strength.

The mean weasel stood between the squirrels and their newfound home—a home they appeared to be willing to defend. Could the stance they were taking in the face of infinite danger be intentional? Did they know what they were doing? Would their lack of experience in confrontation adversely impact them in this major challenge?

This confrontation had the makings of a tremendous learning experience. Maybe, it would be their first and only. They would either succeed in a heroic stand or they would become victims in a horrific failure. Were they willing to roll the dice?

Without any provocation, the weasel suddenly did something uncharacteristic of a weasel: he took a step back. The weasel smiled. It was a smile normally reserved for a long lost friend. Had this nasty weasel met its match? Did he not realize who these three squirrels were? Had Uni, Unkno, and Untra forgotten who they were?

Suddenly and cautiously, the weasel approached Uni, Unkno, and Untra. He offered a hand forward, with a smile now larger than the burrow opening. "How do you do?" said the weasel. "My name is Willie," he added.

The three companions, in what looked like synchronized timing, gave a shocked stare at the weasel. Uncharacteristically, they barraged Willie with questions. "Are you the weasel that left a track of fur rugs, scaring every small animal in this area?" Uni inquired.

Failure is only the opportunity to
begin again more intelligently.

HENRY FORD

"One and the same!" the Willie proudly exclaimed.

"Were you aware of the damage and carnage you left?" Unkno asked.

"I certainly was," Willie answered quickly, so as to leave little time for doubt.

"Is that something you learned to do over time?" Untra asked, as a student might ask a teacher.

"It took me some time to learn how to do it with such precision, but I was a good student. I learned from experience as I moved from region to region," Willie said. "Would you like me to tell you boys a little secret on how I get things done?" Willie left them no choice on whether they wanted to hear what he had to say. Before the shocked squirrels could answer, Willie continued. "I am very adaptable. I can live almost anywhere, and I am fearless. Well, let me say, within reason," he added. "And, because of my size, I can get into most any burrow."

Nodding their heads in comprehension, the three squirrels and their newfound friend nestled next to the tree they could now officially call home. After all, it appeared they had been willing to defend the burrow with their lives. And most would only do that for a home and loved ones.

"So, if I understand you correctly, those traits are intentional," Uni stated.

"Very intentional," Willie quickly replied. "I know I have to do that to not only survive, but also to prosper, because I must eat almost twenty-four hours a day."

"From what you just said, I think we could be in danger of a battle at any moment," Unkno shot back.

"Normally, that would be true, but I am full for the moment. And I pick my battles," answered Willie. "At this moment, I am better off making friends with you guys as opposed to taking on a battle I might not win."

"I imagine that is something you learned the hard way," said Untra, in an accepting, yet inquisitive tone.

"It is something I am still learning," added Willie. "I do not have a history of making friends because I am prone to confrontation. I am attempting to adapt."

"So, you really don't have any fear of anything, nor do you intentionally seek friends?" asked Uni.

"Because of my constant hunger and search for food, I normally have no interest—or the time—to make conversation that does not result in food,"

Willie stated. "I know I should try to stay clear of hawks and eagles," he added.

"How do you know that?" asked Untra. "Did you learn it?"

"I learned the hard way, in a confrontation that almost caused my demise," the weasel stated. "I would love to stay and visit with you guys, but I have to move onto the next territory. I don't have time to waste. I will be getting hungry soon."

The three squirrels and the weasel had reached an uncommon, short-term friendship. It was a friendship that was unlikely to progress to any long-term bond.

Willie promised he would stop and say hi if he ever passed through the area again. He and the squirrels were convinced the chance of that happening was highly unlikely. Willie had to go where he could be assured of an abundant food source. As for the squirrels, they were not sure what the future held for them.

After Willie left, Uni, Unkno, and Untra were feeling good about themselves. They had stood strong together. It was possible their stance was intentional. They might have even known what they were doing. And more importantly, some valuable lessons were

Change comes from
confrontation. You have to be
confronted or confront yourself.

BRYANT MCGILL

learned, even though they came from an unlikely confrontational source.

Uni, Unkno, and Untra had achieved self-awareness. They had come a long way. And at this juncture, one thing was clear: they finally no longer sought to return to Upheaval.

Uni, Unkno, and Untra had earned a little relaxation time to enjoy some fruit and seeds. They settled in their new home to celebrate their majestic achievement.

Unfortunately, this well-earned tranquility did not last long. A loud noise suddenly interrupted them. They did not know what it was. All they knew was it was loud enough to shake the earth around their comfortable home.

Chapter Six

Wheels of Change

Awareness is the first step to
preparation for perpetual change.

As the noise got louder and louder, Uni,
Unkno, and Untra quickly realized it might be pru-
dent to figure out the source. The gradual increase of
the shaking of the ground signaled its fast approach.

As unaccustomed as they were to reflection, the
dramatic confrontation with the weasel had forced
it upon them. In spite of the noise, they could not
help but wonder why the weasel had backed down.
Oddly enough, it may not have been a confrontation

they had sought nor even been willing to engage in. They were not sure.

What did they do that caused the weasel pause? They recognized that they did not knowingly or intentionally confront the weasel. The weasel had obviously perceived the situation differently. Maybe there was something they could take away from that confrontation when they addressed the source of the noise.

The sound of trees falling and branches breaking continued to get louder and louder. A constant buzzing competed for their attention. The ground shook as large trees fell.

The three friends began a cautious walk toward the ruckus. They stopped by a large bush and looked ahead in the distance. What they saw was horrifying. Logs, branches, and leaves were piled high. In between was nothing but a large swath of stumps and scarred earth for as far as they could see. Large machines filled the center of the chaos. The ground absorbed the vibration from the massive machines' tires. It was unlike anything they had seen or heard before.

How could this be? wondered the bewildered squirrels. They had just found a new place to reside,

Fear defeats more people than
any other one thing in the world.

WALDO RALPH WALDO EMERSON

Adversity is the mother of progress.

MAHATMA GANDHI

one they were willing to defend—or so it had seemed.

Were these machines intentionally trying to destroy this place? Did the machines know what they were doing? How could they have learned to cause such devastation?

Although the squirrels did not have the answers to these questions, they did have one major revelation: they needed to return to their new home and figure out a plan of action. The good news was that they were actually making the effort to think about their present and their future. Better yet, they had left apathy in their past. They knew this to be true, because before leaving Upheaval, they would not have been concerned about what lie ahead.

Although Uni, Unkno, and Untra were new to assessment, evaluation, preparation, and planning, they had learned much in the last four days. They thought they had left Upheaval; they did not want to find it again.

Would their newfound awareness, concern, and desire for preparation make a difference?

As they walked home, pondering what they should do, the sounds of motors and falling trees intensified.

Chapter Seven

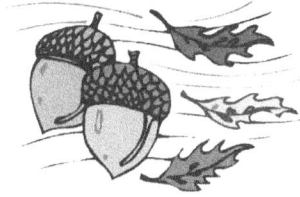

Fork in a Bumpy Road

The success of choosing the right road is
most often defined by our method of travel.

After returning home, Unkno spoke first.
"Based on what we have seen, I think we should
gather some food and create a plan to protect our
home in case that chaos makes its way here."

"You can count on me," Untra enthusiastically
exclaimed. "I'll start looking for food and some
branches to strengthen our home."

"I will do what I have to do," Uni stated with
conviction.

The strength of the team is each individual member. The strength of each member is the team.

PHIL JACKSON

The squirrels left the safety of their burrow to gather nuts, berries, branches, and even stones. They wanted to be prepared for what appeared to be an almost certain onslaught of machinery coming their way. Unlike the apathetic squirrels who had lived for years in Upheaval, these residents of Oodles were not only formulating a plan, they were trying to implement one.

After several hours of gathering food and supplies, they sat down to have a meeting to evaluate what had been accomplished and, more importantly, to determine what yet remained to be done. One major problem was clear: time was not on their side.

"If there is one thing I have learned, we need immediate help to accomplish what needs to get done in the next day," Unkno stated with a sense of urgency.

Without discussing what Unkno had stated, the three squirrels stood up, nodded their heads in agreement, and left their burrow. The destination they needed to reach was obvious to all of them. They needed help—and they needed it now.

Lack of discussion was certainly not unusual for these three squirrels, but what was remarkable was them having a consensus on direction of any kind. And it was becoming clear that the emergence of

Unkno's leadership skills had put him in the position of leader of this small group.

It was a two-hour roundtrip to their destination; which gave them one day to complete their plan to save their home and prepare for what they knew was coming. They were tired, but there was no time to waste.

When they neared the riverbank where they had seen the beavers, they heard the sound of running water and teeth gnawing on wood. These noises were no match for the destruction taking place in Oodles.

Uni, Unkno, and Untra knew they had to talk to the beavers to learn what might help them save their home. Unkno stood up and approached the beavers, his purple stripe lighting up the area and drawing their immediate attention. "Hello. We have been admiring your diligent work and we wondered if you might give us a little of your valuable time. We'd like some advice," Unkno said with much respect in his voice.

"We are busy right now, as you can see. But we would be willing to sit for a few minutes to see if we can be of any help," said Eager, the busiest beaver. He appeared to be the leader of the group.

Coming together is a beginning,
staying together is progress, and
working together is success.

HENRY FORD

Courage is what it takes to stand up and speak; courage is also what it takes to sit down and listen."

WINSTON CHURCHILL

Unkno, Uni, and Untra introduced themselves to the beavers as they all sat down near the shore of the stream. After a short discussion, the squirrels thanked the beavers for their time and advice. Their hope was they had learned enough to face and survive the challenge that was ahead.

After a long day, the threesome returned home. They were exhausted. Unfortunately, it sounded like the machines had made it closer to their home while they were gone. Tired or not, it was time to get to work. There was simply no time to waste.

They realized that things had accelerated much quicker than they had anticipated. Although dusk was approaching, there would be no time for sleep. Sleep would have to wait. After all the years of living in Upheaval, they had finally arrived at a point where they were trying to be aware, learn, and meet life's challenges. Was it too little too late? Time would certainly tell.

Unkno, Untra, and Uni worked throughout the night. It was long night, and too short of a night at the same time. Too soon the sun began to rise in the east. The gradual light on the horizon meant the time of reckoning was not too far off.

The three squirrels collapsed at the base of their home. Fast approaching was the sound of machinery, falling trees, and the vibration of the earth from the unrelenting aggression.

Did these squirrels underestimate the damage and destruction they might have to confront by staying in Oodles? Had they done enough to survive the onslaught? Chaos was at their doorstep. It was loud. It was frightening.

The only war is within. When you are ready to fight it, the field awaits.

AGNOSTIC ZETETIC

Chapter Eight

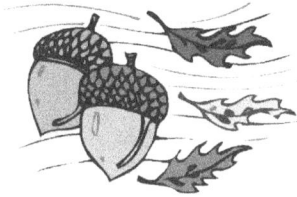

A DEVELOPMENTAL DEMOLITION

**The winds of change
can create major destruction.**

The village of Oodles was no more. What remained was the deafening sound of silence. There were no chirping birds. There was no sound of animals scurrying about. It was barren. It was empty. It was a war zone. The ground had been completely leveled. The only sign of life was ants crawling on the debris.

No longer was there a sign that a weasel had ever been in the area because the fur rugs were nowhere to be seen. There were no sign that healthy, mature trees had ever grown here. There were no bushes or undergrowth for food and protection.

Oodles was a ghost town. This wonderful village, once an abundant home for many, had become a distant memory.

Two hours away, the beavers worked in earnest. Oblivious to the destruction of Oodles, they were busy gathering food and enlarging their home. They were doing the necessary work to prepare for winter.

Farther way, young rats chased each other by the stream while the adult rats continued their hunt for fish.

Unaware of how close they had come to chaos and destruction, the beavers and rats happily went about their business, without a care in the world. They still had to be attentive to the occasional snake or large bird that might cause them harm. But harm and total destruction are two different things. Sometimes combining a little luck with hard work is good.

It is not the strongest of the species that survives, nor the most intelligent that survives. It is the one that is most adaptable to change.

CHARLES DARWIN

Appendix

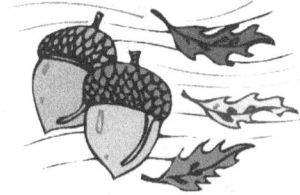

BUSINESS AND LIFE MESSAGES

This appendix provides an overview of the
life and business messages in each chapter.

Chapter One—"Upheaval Revisited"

In this chapter, the three squirrels realize that apathy
and lack of direction are not serving them well. They see
that having no plan of action can actually be a plan—
and a bad one at that.

Life Example:

My first position upon graduating from college was
as an Assistant Manager for a national finance company. After only ten months, I realized this was in a

stagnant situation. I was going nowhere. I recognized that even though I was dedicated to my responsibilities, I respected but disliked working for my supervisor.

My wife and I decided that after our one year wedding anniversary and near my one year job anniversary it was time to go in a new direction. The changes we would make were dramatic. We would move from our home state of Michigan to California. Since I was working for a national company, and had a good work record, I was in a position to request a transfer. The request was accepted, but not promised.

We were in major risk territory. It was only a week before we left when I was notified by the company a position was awaiting me in Southern California. I did not know specifically where or who I might be reporting to. It would have been much easier for me to stagnate as opposed to taking a major risk of uprooting and moving across country.

In California, my career blossomed. After achieving two significant promotions, I had within my sights a district manager position. I also had regional vice-president aspirations. Corporate management reaffirmed those aspirations as real and attainable.

In California we purchased a home. We also had a busy social life that included many friends. The timeout and risk had been well worth the rewards.

Too many people only do what they need to survive. There are times when significant change is necessary, not only for progress, but also survival. As the squirrels, you must believe you can always have an impact on your present and your future. You need to continually evaluate and look forward.

Business Example:

It is not uncommon for business professionals to go through the motions, fall into a pattern, and just take things as they come. The word for this is complacency. Unfortunately, that approach can have major consequences; and worse yet, produce perpetual pitfalls, including the inability to meet new business challenges and business failure.

Challenges will always exist. A challenge can be in the form of working with difficult supervisors and coworkers, tough tasks, or significant career-altering events. Business, industry changes, and competition will always be an evolving process that you will need to stay ahead of. Circuit City, Borders, Nokia, Motorola, and daily newspapers are good examples of those businesses that did not look ahead and make the necessary changes.

On a personal note, my wife and I, and our two young daughters, left Southern Michigan in the early 1980s to move to Northern Michigan. I took a position as a Business Manager for a local television station. I liked and respected the General Manager I reported to. I would learn much from him. This position and timing would open a tremendous opportunity for me. I had planned for this opportunity, and was ready when major turmoil within the station created an opening for me. The business needed a new leader, and I was willing and ready.

Chapter Two—"A Little Rat ... ionality"

In this chapter, the squirrels realize that in order to execute a plan they must first be open to learning. They recognize that they can learn a lot from observation and paying attention.

Life Example:

The lesson is twofold. First, you can learn a lot by observing individuals who have had success and enjoy what they do. Secondly, the best way to get good results is to have a passion for what you do, no matter what it is.

Another important point is that observation without absorption and implementation advances nothing. It is too easy to think that we know everything we need to know. Don't let pride get in the way of learning.

It is also possible to learn how not to do something from someone. Lessons come in many forms.

Business Example:

Most businesses focus on the present and spend little time looking forward. It is this focus on current demands that can result in a business awakening one morning to a dramatically changed industry or economic environment. Catch-up mode is never a good position to be in.

Calling a timeout to evaluate and observe is always just a starting point for a business. It is critical to both business survival and growth to always be looking ahead. Good observation and evaluation today, combined with focus on the future, is paramount to meeting changes and challenges down the road.

Looking forward is the only way a business can navigate ahead of the curve and avert constantly being in catch-up mode. Questions must be asked. Could bookstores have been better prepared for the major impact of the internet and telecommunication technology? Could they have gotten ahead of the curve?

What if the newspaper industry had gotten ahead of consumers' transitioning to the internet for getting their news? What if newspapers had gradually reduced their dependency on classified revenue and hardcopy circulation readership?

What if brick-and-mortar retails had gotten ahead of the consumer shift to internet purchasing?

Chapter Three—"Eye See"
In this chapter, the three squirrels learn that by having their minds open to their surroundings opens their eyes to new awareness. They also begin to learn the importance of taking risks in order to move forward.

Life Example:

Everyone can learn something from another person. For example, the ability of a baby boomer and millennial to communicate well can only result from both taking the time to look, listen, and respect each other.

The other lesson in this chapter is the importance of taking a risk. Taking a risk is not easy; it can make you feel vulnerable. It may seem easier to hold onto the status quo, but getting ahead is only accomplished by challenging the status quo.

Business Example:

Awareness is one of the most important qualities you can possess to be successful. Awareness comes from good observation habits and listening to others.

As business professionals we sometimes become so focused on the immediate that we miss out on what is happening around us. We need to constantly remind ourselves of the importance of listening to colleagues and clients. It is too easy to just talk over others, and think more about our response as opposed to what others are trying to convey. A self-absorbed approach to communication impacts relationships, awareness, knowledge, and sales.

How many times do we walk by something we pass by daily and not recognize a significant change has taken place? How many times do we leave key factors out of a business strategy that are staring us in the face? Taking the time to stop, look, and evaluate can be the difference between success and failure.

I often wonder how many industries and businesses could have averted failure or extinction if their leaders had listened to front-line managers and staff. Were there bookstore and newspaper employees who offered suggestions for meeting the challenges and changes posed by the internet? I have to believe so.

Sometimes business management only sees what it wants to see.

Chapter Four—"Alter the Damn Surroundings"

In this chapter, the three squirrels teach us that we should always be alert to warning signs of a pending change, and that we must create the environment we wish to live in. Additionally, for survival and success, we must perpetually improve what we are given—always work toward a higher level.

Life Example:

In the early 1980s I was managing an office for a national finance company. The business was doing well and I had received three promotions over a three-year period. In October 1979, the Bankruptcy Act of 1978 took effect.

This law caused many finance companies to close, including mine. This was a huge warning sign that I did not pay attention to. If I had realized the impact it would have, I would have redefined my career before I was forced to in 1982.

Business Example:

Circuit City, Borders, and Hollywood Video are companies that were not alert to the warning signs. As a result, they made little effort to change their business models. They are also examples of businesses that could have taken their business model to another level. Alliances may have impacted their survival; and may have also helped them prosper.

Circuit City's strength was its in-store customer service. They provided customers the opportunity to touch products before buying them. They then diminished that model in order to cut costs by replacing skilled personnel with lessor-skilled employees.

Borders could have acknowledged the coming impact of digital technology and the internet. They could have prepared for these changes and enhanced their product offerings to meet the changing marketplace.

Chapter Five—"Standing Tall"

In this chapter, the squirrels learn that in order to overcome a challenge, one must first be willing to confront it. And that a secret to survival is understanding your needs, strengths, and weaknesses.

Life Example:

I have learned that letting a negative situation fester and grow, while simply hoping it will go away, never works. Confrontation is always inevitable. I realized, over time, that confidence in dealing with difficult situations can only come from experience. Positive results do not always happen, but confidence and increased experience working through difficult situations helps.

Business Example:

A good example of a company that has confronted perpetual challenges by looking at "where the puck is going" is Netflix. Netflix seems to understand its strengths and weaknesses at any given time, and has the ability to adjust accordingly.

Initially, Netflix competed with brick-and-mortar video stores by offering delivery of DVDs through the mail. Video streaming, which allowed consumers to watch movies through their tablets and smart phones, was the next technology to come along. Netflix confronted this challenge by getting into licensing shows. They were then able to compete with cable and network TV.

Netflix found an answer at every challenge. Unlike bookstores and daily newspapers, Netflix found answers that would keep them in business.

Chapter Six—Wheels of Change"

In this chapter, the three squirrels quickly realize they will have little time to celebrate their victory. They are immediately confronted with a fast-approaching problem that can only go one direction—from bad to worse.

The lesson here is clear. In life and in business, perpetual change is a given. You must always be prepared for the next challenge awaiting on the horizon. Being combat-ready can be the difference between success and failure.

In the words of the great hockey player Wayne Gretzky: "A good hockey player plays where the puck is. A great hockey player plays where the puck is going to be."

Life Example:

When one crisis, change, or challenge has been taken care of, new changes are already waiting in line. This is the perpetual motion of life. The key to working through this is anticipation, preparation, and a realistic perspective.

Business Example:

An example of continual change and challenges in the business world is the wireless industry. Initially the major challenge was the high number of competitors and the cost of constructing towers. This challenge was replaced by the demand for better signal quality and capacity. The costs of providing better quality and capacity resulted in large companies swallowing up smaller ones.

In spite of lacking the geographical and financial capacity of large companies, some smaller companies stayed the course. They refused to acknowledge the obvious—and paid the ultimate price. They did not survive.

Other small companies saw the handwriting on the wall. They realized they would never have the resources to keep up with the increasing costs of competing. Those small companies, while celebrating their successes, made plans to get out while they could. They could see the wheels of change on the horizon and they benefited financially as a result of having a good exit strategy.

Chapter Seven—"Fork in a Bumpy Road"
In this chapter, Uni, Unkno, and Untra exhibit the importance of capability and the collaboration of skills to prepare for and combat a challenge.

Life Example:

The skills for overcoming major obstacles are not learned overnight and not simply from observing others who possess those skills. Sometimes you need a partner who can add the skills and capability necessary to complement what you possess.

Business Example:

Apple and AT &T partnering to provide the iPhone is a perfect example of what can be accomplished by businesses collaborating to achieve an end. This is a relationship of collaboration at its best in terms of creating an end product.

Chapter Eight—"A Developmental Demolition"

In this chapter, we are left wondering if the three squirrels have done enough to survive the onslaught.

Life and Business Example:

The lesson for life and business is that change can bring you to your knees. It can ultimately destroy a business if wrong decisions are made in this process. Knowing when to prepare, what to prepare for, and when to change direction can have a consequential impact and affect your chances of survival.

About the Author

Michael Khouri's business career spans over forty years managing in many industries that include working regional operations through mergers, acquisitions, restructuring, and growth transitions. He is the Chief Operating Officer/ Executive VP for a Michigan commercial real estate company, and President of MDK Business Solutions. He previously served as a broadcast television ABC Affiliate and NBC Affiliate VP/General Manager and CellularOne Wireless General Manager.

Khouri delivers professional development and motivational presentations to local, regional, and national companies on how to take control in business and in life as opposed to just taking what comes.

OTHER BOOKS BY MICHAEL D. KHOURI

The Power of Ownership: It is simply a matter of choice—Book 1 of the In A Nutshell Series

This book introduces the three squirrels from Upheaval—Uni, Unkno, and Untra—who show us why we should take control in business and in life, and the importance of taking ownership in everything we do. The Business and Personal Messages in this book are:

- Own what you do
- Adversity, obstacles, and change are a given in business and in life
- Recognize the warnings of change and challenge ahead before they arrive
- Teamwork is a must for any business entity to succeed
- Dedication and purpose impact your chances of success
- Always try to take your processes and effort to the next level
- There is no place for complacency
- Be ready to adapt
- Prepare for opportunity and you will recognize it when it arrives

15 Ways to Own Your Future:
Life-Impacting Ways to Create Success and
Enjoyment in Your Business and Personal Life. Take
Control as Opposed to Just Taking What Comes!

Although this was just published in August 2016 by John Hunt Publishing, this book laid the groundwork for the In a Nutshell Series, The Power of Ownership. It is the original format for a seminar Michael has presented to local, regional, and national businesses since 2005. The 15 Ways in this book will help you:

- Take collaboration to another level
- Improve work/life integration
- Make your business and personal world a better place
- Take the "job" out of work

Coming Soon ...

*The Power of Ownership Book 1
of the In a Nutshell Series—Second Edition*

*The Power of Ownership Book 3
of the In a Nutshell Series*

*The Power of Ownership Book 4
of the In a Nutshell Series*

mdkhouri@gmail.com

michaelkhouri.com